STRATEGIC WARFARE

Five Steps to Defeat the Enemy

BY
MARCUS HAYES

STRATEGIC WARFARE
Published by Watersprings Publishing, a division of Watersprings Media House, LLC.
P.O. BOX 1284
Olive Branch, MS 38654
www.waterspringsmedia.com
Contact publisher for bulk orders and permission requests.

Copyrights © 2019 by Marcus Hayes

All rights reserved. No part of this publication may be reproduced, distributed, or transmitted in any form or by any means, including photocopying, recording, or other electronic or mechanical methods, without the prior written permission of the publisher, except in the case of brief quotations embodied in critical reviews and certain other noncommercial uses permitted by copyright law.

Scripture quotations marked "NKJV" are taken from the New King James Version. Copyright © 1982 by Thomas Nelson, Inc. Used by permission. All rights reserved.

Scripture quotations credited to NASB are from the New American Standard Bible, copyright © 1960, 1962, 1963, 1968, 1971, 1972, 1973, 1975, by the Lockman Foundation. Used by permission.

Printed in the United States of America.

Library of Congress Control Number: 2019916503

ISBN-13: 978-1-948877-34-3

STRATEGIC WARFARE

Five Steps to Defeat the Enemy

TABLE OF CONTENTS

	Introduction	7
STEP 1	Choice	12
STEP 2	Submission	20
STEP 3	Identify Your Attack	29
STEP 4	Armor of God	36
STEP 5	The Holy Spirit	48
	Conclusion	53
	Scripture References	54
	About the Author	55

INTRODUCTION

My experience with spiritual warfare began in January 2017. I had always had a fear of death since I could remember, due to a traumatic experience when I was three years old. My father and I were asleep in the living room while my sister and brothers where asleep with my mom in my parent's room. I woke up having to use the restroom, but my father didn't answer me when I asked him to take me. I went to my mother and told her that I had to use the restroom and she took me. After using the restroom, I turned and told my mother that daddy won't wake up. My mom began to tell me that he is just tired because we kept him up at night. My mom went into the living room and found my father dead because of a heart attack in his sleep, this was in 1989.

Fast-forward to 2017 the only man in my life who would tell me that he loved me was my uncle Bobby. At the end of January 2017, my uncle suffered from an aneurysm to the brain which caused a major stroke. He was flown to the hospital unresponsive. My family came to the hospital to see what was going on and this was the first time that I saw life and death in one body. When I went to touch him the left side of his body was normal but when I went to the right side it was already in rigor mortis. My mother was looking at me almost as if she was waiting for me to tell her whether he would make it or not. I knew that half of his body was already dead and that he wasn't going to make it.

One week later we had the funeral and I thought I was fine. That night I went to sleep, and it began. I began to have dreams that I was dying. The dreams began to happen every night and would transfer from me dying to my family dying in the dreams. I would see my wife or my children dying these vivid deaths. About a month later the dreams turned into thoughts and visions while I was awake. I was afraid and had really bad anxiety. The visions started to change and would play out as if I was the one killing myself and killing my family. I decided that it was time to go to a doctor and get help because it had been about three months of thoughts and visions.

I went to the doctor and explained what was happening and the doctor looked at me and said that I was experiencing grief. I was confused. When you think of grief, I imagined something different, like being sad and wanting to have another chance with the person who has passed away, not what I was experiencing. Two months had passed and I was still going through the same thing. When it all started I was 227 pounds and in the first three weeks, I went down to 190 pounds because I wasn't able to eat. The thoughts of suicide and my family dying began to cripple me. After talking with my wife, mom, and sister it was suggested that I get a therapist. The thought of getting one scared me. Although I never wanted to commit the acts, explaining them to a therapist made me feel that I was going to be locked up in a padded room for just thinking them.

When God has you, He protects you while allowing the devil to think that he is winning. I found a therapist in Nashville who had his own practice and I began going to sessions. During the first session I told him everything that was going on, and while nervous about his reaction, there was a peace in me that settled my nerves. After explaining, the first thing he said to me was, "You're not crazy, God has just placed something in you that the devil wants to kill. The design of the attack is to make you feel crazy so that you will kill yourself."

I admit it, that was heavy and a little too much for me. He then began to teach me how to fight with the Word of God to overcome the attacks. Once I had a dream, a lady whose face I could not see said to me that she knew everything, and that God had called me. I began to cry, and I wanted her to stay because I was afraid. The next day I went to work and three of my friends came to my job with the same message. The message they told me was that they have always looked up to me and that they knew the devil had me under water where I couldn't find my feet, and that they wouldn't be surprised if I became a pastor.

Boom, there was my confirmation that God was calling me into ministry. That was important because the night before my father died, he anointed my brother Michael and I, saying that part of him was in both of us. God would then speak to me as clear as day and tell me that He has called me to speak against these spirits. God told me that many of my children are listening to this voice and perceiving it to be themselves. God would tell me that these spirits have no power and are trying to get you to do something that they cannot do. This was in 2017 when the number of mass killings and the suicide rate was high. God would then show me through the Bible how Jesus would respond to these spirits. God gave me five steps that the world needs to know in order to overcome spiritual battles. I am here today because I know it works.

STEP 1

CHOICE

In life we are all faced with decisions to choose something every day, choices to do right and choices to do wrong, choices to go left and to go right, choices to participate in something or not. Every choice we make leads us in the direction we all would like to go. These choices are the beautiful gift that God gave us as humans. The same is true in spiritual warfare.

Have you ever been told when facing any battle that God just needs you to stand? What does that mean, how do I stand against Satan who is bigger and stronger? When I asked God how to stand, He gave me five steps that I would need to be able to stand and get the victory in my battle. The first thing God told me to do was to make a choice. Before Jesus began His ministry there were five specific things that He did to show us what to do, not only in life, but when engaging in spiritual warfare.

While the Word was being spread through John the Baptist in Matthew 3, Jesus showed us what must happen in order for us to walk in the divine order of God. Jesus comes on the scene and before speaking He does something with His actions. Jesus makes a public decision to confirm everything John the Baptist was preaching, that the kingdom of heaven is at hand. Jesus makes a choice by being baptized by John. The choice that Jesus makes lets us know that in our life there is a huge decision to be made, and that is to make a choice.

Every day in our lives we make choices, choices to turn right and choices to go left. Our choices can lead us to our desired route or on a detour. It is the same in spiritual warfare, a choice has to be made. In the beginning, God created the whole world with the intention to have a relationship with all things. He made the sun the moon and the stars to declare His Glory, but when He made man and angels He gave them something that no other creation had. The man and angels had the ability to make choices on what to do and what not to do. It has been said that the angels were created when God created the heavens and earth. Although the Bible doesn't say specifically when, the question that would be asked is what did the angels have to choose from since it was only God and them. I have asked this question as well, and when I look at what happens to Lucifer, I see what the choice was.

EZEKIEL 28:16 NKJV
"By the abundance of your trading you became filled with violence within, and you sinned."

Lucifer makes a trade, he was internally filled with violence and sin. The choice was to choose God or himself. The trade that Lucifer made was to trade truth for a lie. He chose to believe himself over the truth that was right in front of him. In Isaiah 14:13 NKJV, we see what Lucifer said to himself, *"I will ascend to heaven and raise my throne above the stars of God."* In this text,

Strategic Warfare

Lucifer is in Eden and wants to be above God so much so that he tells himself how to get there. Lucifer was over the very presence of God and was face to face with the truth. Then Lucifer goes and persuades other angels to make the same decision. This is how we see a choice changed the world.

By the time Adam and Eve come on the scene, there is another choice that comes into existence. Satan had already made his choice and now that God has made man and woman he wants to corrupt the man that was made in God's image. This is all important when it comes to spiritual warfare. By understanding the beginning we may know how much power our choices have. In spiritual warfare, there are two spirits that are trying to occupy you. This is why understanding the beginning and what we are choosing helps us when finding ourselves in spiritual warfare. God is the Author of all, the Alpha and Omega the Beginning and the End. God is the Creator of all and has a plan for every one of our lives.

God's plan is to give us eternal life with Him, while Satan is here to provide the plan of eternal death. Then the question is, what is spiritual warfare? Spiritual warfare is when two spirits are at war to occupy you. To understand this, we must understand our role in this war.

2 CORINTHIANS 4:7 NKJV
"But we have this treasure in earthen vessels, that the excellence of the power may be of God and not us."

The author Paul is telling us that our bodies are a vessel, and a vessel is created to be filled. Our role is to choose which spirit will occupy our bodies, and for that to happen we must all make a choice of whether we will choose God or Satan. We are to choose the truth or to make a trade for the truth for a lie like Lucifer did, when he chose himself.

The feeling of knowing what is right but making a conscious choice for what is wrong, is making a trade for what is true. It is the same as knowing that stealing is not right, but

Strategic Warfare

then trading that truth for a lie because of our circumstance. Nothing in this world, or out of this world, can force itself upon you. If you are possessed, you must make a choice within yourself to allow whatever it is to possess you. There is power in your choice. Humans are the only species on earth that have the ability to choose, you don't see a fish choosing not to swim or a tree choosing not to produce oxygen. Your choice has power.

In Joshua 24:15 NKJV, *"and if it seems evil to you to serve the Lord, choose for yourselves this day whom you will serve, whether the gods which your fathers served that were on the other side of the River, or the gods of the Amorites, in whose land you dwell. But as for me and my house, we will serve the Lord."* The text tells us to choose ye this day in whom you will serve because your choice will be honored by God. Making your choice to allow God to occupy you is the first step in the war. This doesn't mean that the devil will disappear, but it does mean that you have established which side you will stand on. When making the choice on which side you're on you are now engaging in the war, and the fight is on. It is no longer a bully beating you up with no blows thrown from you. You have now landed your first punch by making a choice to choose God. The fight that we have in a spiritual battle is making decisions, this is the wrestle that we see in Ephesians 6:12 KJV, which says, *"We wrestle not against flesh and blood, but against principalities, against powers, against the rulers of the darkness of this world, against spiritual wickedness in high places."* The beginning of the text lets us know that there is a part of the battle that we all participate in, which is to wrestle. This means that you have a role to play in the spiritual battle over your life, and it starts with your choice. The battle is the Lords', but we have to choose God to see the victory in the war. Jesus is our example, and the first thing that we all must do is make the choice to follow God the same way that He did.

While you may be in a spiritual attack right now, it is important that you make your choice known to God and Satan so that there is a clear understanding who you are with.

To do this, say the following aloud: God I choose You this day and I confess with my mouth as a

Strategic Warfare

declaration that I am Yours and will stand with You until the end.

STEP 2

SUBMISSION

According to Merriam Webster Dictionary, the meaning of submission is an act of submitting to the authority or control of another. I would suggest to you that in spiritual warfare the definition would simply mean to agree. In spiritual warfare, there are two spirits that want to occupy you. For Christians to submit is to release your control, which in turn means faith. When it comes to spiritual warfare both God and Satan have a mission that each one wants you to sub or agree to. When the devil is attacking you, there is a purpose that he wants to accomplish. There is a mission. For the mission to be accomplished you have to submit and agree to it.

Submitting to God is accepting the things

that you cannot change. Isaiah 55:8 NKJV says, *"For my thoughts are not your thoughts, neither are your ways my ways, declares the Lord."* Submission says in every circumstance, not my will, but thy will be done. When we submit to God, God says the same thing He told Jeremiah in verse 29:11 NKJV, *"For I know the thoughts that I think toward you, saith the Lord, thoughts of peace, and not of evil, to give you an expected end."* God is saying I have a mission for your life, and I want you to know that it takes submission to accomplish it. God's plan for our lives is far better than anything that we can imagine. When we submit, we are saying God have Your way in my life. Like a father who wants to see his son or daughter succeed, how much more does our heavenly Father want to bless us daily. God is a God of order, even during a spiritual attack. When God created the heavens and the earth it happened in order.

2 Timothy 1:7 KJV
"For God has not given us the spirit of fear; but of power, and of love, and a sound mind. This verse lets us know that our mind is to never be in a state of confusion because God has not given us a mind that is confused."

Strategic Warfare

Genesis 1:11-12 NKJV
"Then God said, Let the earth bring forth grass, the herb yielding seed, and the fruit tree yielding fruit after his kind, whose seed is in itself, upon the earth: and it was so. And the earth brought forth grass, and herb yielding seed after his kind, and the tree yielding fruit, whose seed was in itself, after his kind: and God saw that it was good."

Why would God make grass, herbs, and trees that had fruit if no one was there? It was because of order. So, when He created man there would be no reason for the man to go without. If I were God, which I wouldn't want to be, I would have created Adam first and then allowed him to see everything that I created with my words. But Gods way was best for us. If He did it my way, faith would not have the same meaning.

Gods ways are perfect! His way has no flaws, even when thinking in our small brains that there is a better way. James 4:7 NASB says, *"Submit unto the Lord, resist the devil, and he will flee from you."* There is order in the text, the first thing that the text tells us is to submit unto God. When we submit to God that doesn't mean that the attacks will stop, it means that you trust God for allowing it to happen. When we submit to God we are saying, God, I accept that You are all knowing and the Creator of all things. When we submit, we bring forth the relationship of knowing our Creator and His way not only for our lives but for the whole world. Submission looks like us being ok that God allowed the devil to attack us.

Remember that this book is to show how Jesus took each step before He began His ministry of creating the new church. So, in chapter 1 we see Him through Matthew 3:13-17 make the choice to be baptized before even speaking a word. Jesus submits with the very next move that He makes by being led by the Spirit to the wilderness. Matthew 4:1 NASB says, *"Then Jesus was led up by the spirit into the wilderness to be tempted by the devil."* Question, why would Jesus be okay with going on a fast and to meet the devil? I suggest to you that Jesus was giving us an example to make a choice by submitting to the Father."

The decision Jesus makes gives us a manual of what will happen to all of us when we align with divine purpose in our lives. When God has a plan for your life, which we all have, you have to meet the devil the same way Jesus had to meet him before He began his ministry. Meeting the devil doesn't mean that you will see him and have to go toe to toe with him. It does mean that something will start to happen, like doubt, fear, negative or evil thoughts, sickness, the desire to quit, etc.

The devil knows how to attack you, he knows your weakness and how to defeat you when you don't have God on your side.

I would suggest to you that there will be a period before your attack, that God is drawing near to you with signs that we all miss. Jesus simply identifies the signs where the Holy Spirit leads Him and says, Father You know best, so I will go. The biggest mistake we all have made is choosing God, but not submitting to Him. Submission is accepting Gods way and not our own, this means we are Spirit-driven and not flesh-driven. Submission is a requirement in our relationship with Christ.

> ROMANS 16:20 NASB
> *"The God of peace will soon crush Satan under your feet. When under attack we must remind ourselves of this, and Satan, that the fight is fixed."*

When Job was attacked, Job 1:12 lets us know that Satan has to get permission to attack. The same happens to us in spiritual warfare, when the devil starts the attack on your life, just remember he had to get permission. That means that God has already set the way of escape, so that we may have the victory. Now I know that the question will arise in us, why is God allowing this to happen when we are His children? I have asked the same question to God and He told me, in order for Me (God) to get the victory there has to be a war, and in order for there to be a war, He must have soldiers. God is calling us to fight in a war that He has already won, we are just enduring to the end, to see the Victory. I suggest

Matthew 4:5 NASB
"When the devil takes Jesus up to the Holy City and stood him on the pinnacle of the temple and said to Him if you are the Son of God, throw yourself down and the angels will take charge over you."

to you that this is the defining moment when we all must submit to God. Jesus went through it to give us the answer sheet to conquer the devil. Each blow that the devil throws at you will hurt but God uses that to strengthen you. So let the punches come, we will be stronger in the end when we align ourselves with God by submitting to Him.

STEP 3

IDENTIFY YOUR ATTACK

The biggest blow that the devil can throw at you is confusion. If the devil can get you confused, then he can get you to make the wrong decision to accomplish his mission in your life. This is why it is important that you identify the root of your attack. The worst fight to be in is the fight that you didn't know you were in. To feel punches hit you, but not know who is throwing them and where they are coming from is the main component that the devil uses to accomplish his mission. This is why 2 Timothy 1:7 KJV says, "For God has not given us the spirit of fear; but of power, and of love, and a sound mind. This verse lets us know that our mind is to never be in a state of confusion because God has not given us a mind that is confused." So, confusion is from the devil in spiritual warfare.

When God created the world, He gave everything something special that others didn't have. He gave the lion power, strong jaws and teeth. He gave the cheetah speed; the lizard camouflage, capability to hide. He gave the birds wings to fly; the trees the ability to give oxygen; fish the ability to breathe underwater.

The question is, what did He give us as humans? He gave us a brain; the brain is so complex that even in 2019 we still don't understand fully the capabilities the brain has and how it fully works. According to the New Scientist website, the brain is the most intricate organ in the human body. It produces our every thought, action, memory, feeling, and experience of the world. The brain is a jelly-like mass of tissue, weighing in at around 3 pounds, contains a staggering one hundred billion nerve cells, or neurons. The complexity of the connectivity between these cells is mind-blowing. Each neuron can make contact with thousands, or even tens of thousands of others via tiny structures called synapses. Our

Strategic Warfare

brains form a million new connections for every second of our lives. The pattern and strength of the connections are constantly changing, and no two brains are alike.

The mind is where the battlefield is for spiritual warfare. The devil attacks the memory, imagination, and feelings. One of the biggest ways the devil attacks us is in our emotions and feelings.

EZEKIEL 28:16 NASB
"By the abundance of your trade, You were internally filled with violence, and you sinned; therefore I have cast you as profane, from the mountain of God. And I have destroyed you, O covering cherub. From the midst of the stones of fire. The devil makes the trade for the truth for a lie that he can be better at being God than God."

Every time we go through anything in life we are trying to control the feelings that happen within us. Feelings that makes us want to give up and quit, feelings of why me, feelings of depression, worry, and anxiety about something we can't control. When the devil can get us in our feelings, and away from rational thoughts he can present the lie for us to choose.

We are all in a daily battle of wanting to have the truth but that doesn't mean that the lie will not be presented for us to choose and agree (submit) to. We see this action in every sin someone commits, (lust, adultery, murder, stealing, homosexuality, addiction, idolatry, abuse of others, etc.). And as we can see in the world today, the devil has done a great job at confusing us. God is raising up a generation that will attack and identify this snare and will overcome it and want to live Holy.

After overcoming one sin it seems as though it gets harder for us with something else. Watch what Jesus says about unclean spirits in Matthew 12:43-45 NKJV, *"when an unclean spirit goes out of a man, he goes through dry places, seeking rest, and finds none. Then he (the spirit) says I will return to my house from which I came. And when he comes, he finds it empty, swept, and put in order. Then he goes and takes with seven other spirits more wicked than himself, and they*

Strategic Warfare

enter and dwell there, and the last state of that man is worse than the first. So, shall it be with this wicked generation?"

In the text, we see victory and loss. The man has overcome one spirit, but seven more wicked spirits came with the one that he overcame. The issue here is that the man, although overcoming the one spirit, didn't replace the evil spirit with another spirit. So, when the spirit came back the house (which is himself) it is clean but is still vacant. This ties to steps one and two, which are to choose and submit. Identifying what's happening will help us understand the spirits that want to occupy us. This is why a person can be free from sin like lust but then can become addicted to drugs. What happens is the spirit within has not been replaced with God.

The biggest example that we can use to identify our attacks is through the life of Jesus. In Matthew 4:1-11, Jesus is attacked with various temptations in which He identifies the root before responding to the devil. To be tempted means to entice, to do wrong by promise of pleasure or gain. Sin comes from a legitimate need inside of us. Sin is the opposite of good but is obtained by evil which is against the order of God. So, when Jesus is faced with the first temptation of turning the stones into bread, the fact is Jesus knew that God would provide, and has cattle on a thousand hills, and can rain manna down to feed Him. Jesus' flesh is hungry from the fast, and to get Jesus to break the spiritual connection the devil tempts Him to have a physical connection to food. Jesus understands this and responds to the root of the attack. Matthew 4:5 NASB reads, *"When the devil takes Jesus up to the Holy City and stood Him on the pinnacle of the temple and said to Him if you are the Son of God, throw yourself down and the angels will take charge over you."* Jesus understands that the root of the attack is for Him to commit suicide and to end what God is about to do through Him. When the devil offered Him all the kingdoms of the world if He would bow down and worship Him, Jesus understands the root, which is to worship earthly things and not Godly things.

Just like Jesus, we must all respond the same way when in spiritual warfare with the devil. We must identify the root of why we are being

Strategic Warfare

attacked. The devil is not attacking us, but Who is inside of us, God and His Spirit. So, let's not allow the devil to play with our emotions and feelings about life, and what God has for us. No longer will we allow the devil to play with our imaginations to obtain his goal to keep us in sin and to be away from the presence of God.

STEP 4

ARMOR OF GOD

When the United States is at war, they equip the soldiers with specific attire to wear. The soldiers are given special clothes and weapons to conquer the enemy that they are facing. The clothes given are for times when they are to be visible, and when they need to hide. Their weapons are given to them beforehand, so they can practice how to use them during war. Preparation and armor for war are given to us as Christians as well. The intent of supplying someone with armor is for the person to practice and become effective at using them.

As Christians, God wants us to know that He has left us armor to conquer life and the enemy, Satan. This armor is for defeating and activating

Strategic Warfare

heavenly help in a spiritual battle. Though the battle is the Lords He does require us to put on armor to stand as He fights the battle.

EPHESIANS 6:10-18 NKJV
*gives us what to put on in this war.
"Finally, my brethren, be strong in the Lord and in the power of His might. Put on the whole armor of God, that you may be able to stand against the wiles of the devil. For we do not wrestle against flesh and blood, but against principalities, against powers, against the rulers of the darkness of this age, against spiritual hosts of wickedness in the heavenly places. Therefore take up the whole armor of God, that you may be able to withstand in the evil day, and having done all, to stand. Stand therefore, having girded your waist with truth, having put on the breastplate of righteousness, and having shod your feet with the preparation of the gospel of peace; above all, taking the shield of faith with which you will be able to quench all the fiery darts of the wicked one. And take the helmet of salvation, and the sword of the Spirit, which is the word of God; praying always with all prayer and supplication in the Spirit, being watchful to this end with all perseverance and supplication for all the saints."*

Marcus Hayes

So, the question would be, why would we need armor for a battle that God will fight? Verse 12 tells us that we must understand that we wrestle not against flesh and blood but against rulers of darkness. To wrestle means that there is a part that we play in the war. For God to get the victory there must be a war, and to have a war God must have soldiers. May I suggest that if you are going through a spiritual attack that God is calling you to be a soldier for Him.

I loved to fight growing up. When I was facing my battle, this is what I heard God say to me, and this gave me confidence in Him. God said to me, "instead of fighting your brothers and sisters I'm calling you to fight in a war that saves lives through me (God)."

The next question I asked God was how do I put on this armor and how do I use it? The question was then asked to me by God, if you could only choose one part of the armor which one would you choose? My first answer was the shield to protect myself, because of the saying 'defense is what wins games'. God said all you would be doing is standing there feeling every hit, without being able to respond or counter-

Strategic Warfare

attack. So, the next answer was the sword. If i only had one part of the armor to use it would be the sword so that you can attack and strike. Then it clicked, the sword is the word of God and when I use the word of God the more the other pieces were put on.

When we read the word of God something starts to happen in our life, we start to become more confident and closer to the Creator of the world. The relationship with God starts to grow, and purpose is birthed in our lives.

When you are in the word of God your faith starts to grow, you now have your shield. When you are in the word you start to want to live righteous which is the order of God, you now have your breastplate. When you are in the word you start to despise lies and now you have the belt of truth. When you are in the word there is a peace that comes over you, you start to not be so angry about everything and now you have the shoes of peace on. When you are in the word you start to want to be in His presence daily and long to be with Him and communicate with Him. You now have a relationship, and through the relationship you now have the helmet of salvation.

Paul gives us the parts of the armor and we tend to only look at the 7, but really, he gives us 8. In the last verse, which is 18, he tells us to pray always with all prayer and supplication in the spirit. Praying is what activates the armor when you have put it on. When you pray with the armor of God on you are in order, and in line for God to respond. Your prayer is a prayer that is humble and in full acknowledgment of who God is.

You will know how to call on the name of the Father by the specific needs and desires of your heart. You will call on Elohim when you need His power and might. You will call on Yahweh which means Lord, or the I am. You are saying God You have full control over my life, have Your way with me. You will call on Abba, which means Daddy or Father. And just like your parents who answer you when you call, how much more does God want to answer your prayer. You will call on El Elyon, which means the most-high God and which reminds you that He is above all that you will ever face. You will call on El Roi which means the God who sees, and this reminds you that He sees all, that what you are facing is not unseen. You will call on El Shaddai which means God almighty, He is all powerful and is the Mighty One. You will call on Yahweh Yireh which means the Lord will provide and this reminds you that He will take care of you. You will call on Yahweh Nissi which means the Lord is my banner, God will protect you. You will call on Jehovah Rapha which means the Lord who heals, He will heal you from sickness and blows from the enemy. You will call on Yahweh Shalom which means, The Lord is Peace, He is the giver of peace and will grant you peace in the middle of the storm.

God loves to hear from you and because He gave us specific names to call Him He responds with the direct need that we ask for.

Say this prayer, God although you have allowed the attack to come, I know that the way of escape is through You, so I pray to El Shaddai and Yahweh Shalom for power and peace in this attack.

Everything God showed me in these steps was what Jesus did from being baptized to going into the wilderness. Jesus uses His armor in the wilderness and the main weapon of choice that He shows us is the sword. Let's begin at Matthew 4:3-4 NKJV, and the tempter (who is Satan) came to him, he said, "if you are the Son of God, command that these stones become bread." Jesus used the Word to respond to Satan, He didn't respond with his own intellect or language. Jesus responds using Deuteronomy 8:3 NKJV, which He takes the line that says, "man shall not live by bread alone but by every word that proceeds from the mouth of the Lord." Jesus' response was deeper than the surface presentation that the devil used. Jesus uses this verse to let the devil know that He was chosen by God the same way the Israelites were in Deuteronomy 8:3. The fact is, Jesus needed to eat, but how the devil told Him to obtain the food would have been against God's will, which is a sin. Remember that the Spirit of God leads Jesus to the fast, so breaking the fast outside of God's timing would have been a sin.

The second temptation is in Matthew 4:5-7 NKJV, then the devil took him up into the holy city, set Jesus on the pinnacle of the temple, and said to him, "If you are the son of God, throw yourself down. For it is written: He shall give his angels charge over you, and in their hands, they shall bear you up, Lest you dash your foot against a stone." Jesus again responds with the word, although the devil quoted Psalm 91:11-12, Jesus quotes Deuteronomy 6:16. The presentation that the devil uses is the desire to quit, the devil wanted Jesus to commit suicide because he knew that God did not tell Jesus to throw Himself down. So here it is again, where Jesus has to correct the need of the flesh that wants to give up, and give us an example on how to respond to the devil when he throws snares at us. Jesus responds, *"it is written again, you shall not tempt the Lord Your God."*

I remember in my attack where I thought that I couldn't say this because I am not God. The Holy Spirit came to me and said that I and you have every right to say this to Satan because he is not attacking you, he is wanting to get to God who is in you. When the devil is attacking you, he doesn't go after you, it's the Spirit that is in you that he is going after. Remember that you are a vessel that needs to be filled. Once you have made your choice and submitted to God, you are now occupied and now have a purpose to bring others out of darkness, which takes away from the mission that the devil wants to accomplish.

The third temptation in Matthew 4:8-10 NKJV, *"the devil took Jesus up on an exceedingly high mountain and showed Him all the kingdoms of the world and their glory, and said to Jesus, all these things I will give you if you will fall down and worship me."* Jesus responds with Deuteronomy 6:13 NKJV, *"you shall worship the Lord your God, and Him only you shall serve."* We see this in today's world where the desire to be famous and obtain earthly possessions is more important than the relationship with God. I'm not saying that you are supposed to be poor, but wealth without order will lead to destruction, and then the worship of other things that are not of God.

The desire to be successful will come to all of us, but if it is out of order, and we don't put God first, then we will lose our soul. In Mark 8:36 NKJV Jesus tells us these exact words, *"For what will it profit a man if he gains the whole world and loses his own soul."* The word of God is to be used as a sword in our daily life and when we are faced with spiritual warfare. We have been

Strategic Warfare

called to fight, and we are not fighting naked. We have armor, and to win this war God wants us to use what He equipped us with to overcome the enemy.

Genesis 6:3 NKJV
"My Spirit shall not strive with man forever, for he is indeed flesh; yet his days shall be one hundred and twenty years."

STEP 5

THE HOLY SPIRIT

We are at the last step of what God told me to do in my spiritual attack. The biggest thing that I tell myself and would suggest to you is that these five steps are something that you apply every day. To make a choice, submit, identify the attack, put on the armor, and ask for the Holy Spirit is an active process that we should desire to have daily. Making a decision for Christ is an active choice that we all must make daily so that the world, and the flesh will not win. The last component of standing while in spiritual warfare is the Holy Spirit. The Holy Spirit is the most important part of the steps to stand as a Christian. The Holy Spirit is Who helps you make each step to stand. He enables you and gives you the desire to stand daily.

To get an understanding of who the Holy Spirit is, we must go to how Jesus describes Him.

JOHN 16:5-15 NKJV
"But now I go away to Him who sent Me, and none of you asks Me, 'Where are You going?' But because I have said these things to you, sorrow has filled your heart. Nevertheless, I tell you the truth. It is to your advantage that I go away; for if I do not go away, the Helper will not come to you; but if I depart, I will send Him to you. And when He has come, He will convict the world of sin, and of righteousness, and of judgment: of sin, because they do not believe in Me; of righteousness, because I go to My Father and you see Me no more; of judgment, because the ruler of this world is judged. "I still have many things to say to you, but you cannot bear them now. However, when He, the Spirit of truth, has come, He will guide you into all truth; for He will not speak on His own authority, but whatever He hears He will speak; and He will tell you things to come. He will glorify Me, for He will take of what is Mine and declare it to you. All things that the Father has are Mine. Therefore, I said that He will take of Mine and declare it to you."

Jesus lets us know His characteristics and why He has been here since the death of Christ. Jesus tells us that He will be truthful and will guide us into all truth. Jesus tells us that the Holy Spirit communicates not from His own authority, but He speaks to us what He hears from God and Jesus. This means that if we are to hear from God it will be through Him and Him alone.

The first time before Jesus defines to us who the Holy Spirit is, we see Him in Genesis 1:2 NKJV, "the earth was without form, and void, and darkness was on the face of the deep. And the Spirit of God was hovering over the face of the waters. The next verse God speaks, and things come to form. The Holy Spirit made things happen when the Father spoke. When God said let there be light the Holy Spirit made it happen with the sun and moon. The Holy Spirit creates and finishes the mission of the Father."

In Genesis 6:3 NKJV, and the Lord said, "My Spirit shall not strive with man forever, for he is indeed flesh; yet his days shall be one hundred and twenty years." The key word in the text is that the Holy Spirit will not strive. The meaning of strive is to make a great effort to achieve

Strategic Warfare

something. You may be asking why is this important. Remember, in John 16:8 Jesus says that He convicts us, meaning to make a great effort to achieve Gods goal for our salvation. This is helpful for us to know in our daily life what God is doing, so when under attack we recognize who is speaking. We should be so in-tune with the voice of God that when the devil speaks, we recognize that it's not God. The biggest thing the devil can do is to have us confused about who is speaking in spiritual warfare. The devil wants to confuse our own voice with his and to drown out Gods voice who speaks through the Holy Spirit.

In the Old Testament, we see the Holy Spirit on a different assignment. In the old testament, He was to rest on specific people and individuals. We see this in Numbers 27:18, Moses lays hands on Joshua and the Holy Spirit is upon him. In the new testament, John 16:8 Jesus says, *"and when he has come, He will convict the world of sin, and of righteousness, and of judgement."* The Holy Spirit is now available to everyone who believes and ask for Him. When the Holy Spirit speaks it is with authority that cannot be challenged, not even by the devil. When Jesus is in the wilderness, we must first remember who leads Him to the wilderness, it is the Holy Spirit. So, when Jesus speaks it is with all authority of the Father. So, when the devil is speaking to you, he will never be bothered with your voice because you have no authority. This is why we must ask for the Holy Spirit daily, so when we are under attack or speaking to someone, He has authority.

I would suggest to you that some of the attacks that we encounter with the devil we have been led to by the Holy Spirit. This means no matter what you are going through in your spiritual attack, there is someone called the Holy Spirit who will bring you out and speak with authority to the devil. The Holy Spirit will use your mouth to speak and rebuke the devil away from you. He will strengthen you when you are weak and give you boldness and courage in the midst of your storm. The Holy Spirit is the seal of God. When Jesus comes back He is looking for the ones who allowed the Holy Spirit to occupy their vessel. The Holy Spirit enables you to worship God in spirit and truth because He is the One who reveals all truth. The Holy Spirit transforms your mind and changes your desires

Strategic Warfare

to match the desires of God.

As I conclude, my prayer is that it is clear on what God demands from us to stand against the enemy. To stand means to be on solid ground, and in spiritual warfare the solid ground is Jesus. God is a God of order and even when spiritual warfare happens He still demands order from us. God will never force Himself on us, this is why we must be intentional with choosing Him daily. These steps got me through the worst attacks of my life, and I know it will do the same for you.

God is omni-present and the devil is not, so remember how special you must be in the eyes of God that he had to ask for permission to come to you. And since God knew that he would come, He has already given the way of escape and is with you. Stand in boldness and know that the Holy Spirit is with you and will finish the attack on your life. Jesus is soon to come to finish all evil and honor the choices we have made to stand for Him.

So, now unto Him who is able to keep us from falling, and to present us faultless before the presence of His glory with exceeding joy, to the only wise God our Saviour, be glory and majesty, dominion and power, both now and forever. Amen.

James 4:7 NASB
"Submit unto the Lord, resist the devil, and he will flee from you."

CONCLUSION

Lastly, I want to leave you with scriptures that I spoke over my life when I was under attack. Depending on how I was feeling, I would speak aloud in my room these scriptures. Remember speaking scriptures with your mouth removes evil thoughts, by doing this you are using your sword against the enemy. You can't fight your mind with your mind, your thoughts with your thoughts, you're going to have to open your mouth to speak the word of God to the enemy.

SCRIPTURE REFERENCES

John 11:24-26 NASB, for fear of death.
Roman 16:20 NASB, when you feel an evil presence.
Psalms 18:1-4 NASB, when feeling weak.
Luke 10:19 NASB, for confidence.
James 4:7 NASB, for God's order for victory over the devil.
Zechariah 3:1-2 NASB, for how to rebuke.
1 John 4:4 NASB, reassurance.
Psalms 42:5 NASB, self-check of fear.
Romans 8:28 NASB, for finding purpose in the storm.
Philippians 4:6-7 NASB, for anxious thoughts.
2 Corinthians 10:5 NKJV, to fix imagination.
Psalms 119:66-68 NASB, for perspective.
Psalms 27 NASB, for depression.

ABOUT THE AUTHOR

At the age of 3 Marcus Hayes found his father who had passed away in his sleep from a heart attack. At the age of thirteen Marcus was a youth preacher at New Covenant SDA church in Memphis, Tennessee. He walked away from his calling to pursue other gifts that he possessed at 15. Marcus has worked in many different careers in his life, he has been a manager in the restaurant industry, played the drums for well-known artists, has studied embalming, sung in gospel choirs, and is currently studying Theology at Oakwood University in Huntsville, Alabama. Marcus has a heart to see his generation turn to God and to be saved. Through his interaction with the spiritual realm, he is obedient to God to make sure every person understands how to fight and stand for Christ. Marcus has been through a lot in 33 years but God has been faithful and kept him.

www.ingramcontent.com/pod-product-compliance
Lightning Source LLC
Chambersburg PA
CBHW052106110526
44591CB00013B/2368